PERSONALITY AWARENESS

YOUR PERSONALITY IS THE BLUEPRINT TO YOUR PURPOSE

Copyright ©2025

All Rights Reserved

Table of Contents

Introduction: Why Personality Awareness Matters 1

Chapter 1: Meet Your Autopilot 3

Chapter 2: Meet The Enneagram 6

Chapter 3: Meet Your Inner Counsel – The Heart, Head, and Body, our Centers of Intelligence 9

Chapter 4: Meet Your Personality 15

Chapter 5: Meet Famous Enneagram Personalities from History 22

Chapter 6: Meet Your Purpose 27

Chapter 7: Meet Your Guide for Better Mental Health 33

Chapter 8: Meet the New YOU 2.0 40

Introduction: Why Personality Awareness Matters

Personality Awareness is an exciting and practical tool that opens the door to better self-understanding and deeper, more meaningful relationships. Unlike traditional psychology, which can often seem complex and abstract, Personality Awareness offers straightforward, accessible insights that you can use every day. This book will equip you with the tools to connect and communicate with anyone, all by uncovering the powerful forces driving our behaviors, thoughts, and interactions.

The Practical Power of Personality Awareness

Our personality influences every part of our lives—how we approach challenges, relate to others, and make choices. And yet, many of us go through life unaware of the subconscious drivers shaping our actions and responses. This book, *Personality Awareness*, bridges the gap between the subconscious and conscious mind, helping you recognize the patterns and motivations underlying your personality. With this awareness, you gain the tools to live with greater purpose, intention, and clarity.

A Simplified Path to Self-Understanding

While understanding psychology can feel intimidating, Personality Awareness is designed to be practical and approachable. This is self-knowledge made simple, built for everyday use. By learning this framework, you won't need a deep background in psychology to understand yourself better—you'll just need an interest in using practical insights to live a fuller, healthier life.

The Enneagram: Your Essential Tool

At the core of Personality Awareness is the Enneagram, a personality system that goes beyond surface-level traits to reveal our deeper motivations, fears, and strengths. In this book, you'll gain one of the most comprehensive and practical understandings of the Enneagram, making it useful in every area of life—from personal growth to relationships to career decisions. You'll find that the Enneagram isn't just a way to describe our personality; it's a tool for knowing yourself on a profound level.

Connecting the Subconscious and Conscious Mind

Our personalities emerge from the dynamic interplay between the subconscious mind, which drives our instincts and emotions, and the conscious mind, which governs our intellect and decisions. Personality Awareness connects these two systems, showing you how to work with your natural instincts while also making intentional choices that align with your values and goals. The more aware you become of these forces, the more empowered you are to shape your life purposefully.

The Transformative Journey of Personality Awareness

Learning Personality Awareness has transformed my relationships, especially my marriage. This understanding has given me the tools to connect with my wife more deeply and appreciate the unique ways our personalities interact. It's allowed us to grow closer and communicate better, which has improved not only our marriage but also my relationships with friends, family, and colleagues. I believe that Personality Awareness is the best tool for practical, meaningful insights into any relationship.

A Roadmap to the Essentials of Life

This book is designed as a practical roadmap to the core areas of life that our personality influences. Here's a glimpse of what we'll cover:

- **Chapter 1 - Meet Your Autopilot**: Understanding the automatic side of our mind and its impact on our actions.
- **Chapter 2 - Meet the Enneagram**: Diving into the Enneagram as a practical tool for decoding our personality.
- **Chapter 3 - Meet The Centers of Intelligence- Three Directors of Inner Counsel**: Learning about three primary forces that shape our perspective.
- **Chapter 4 - Meet Your Personality**: Uncovering your unique personality makeup and its influence.
- **Chapter 5 - Meet Famous Enneagram Personalities from History**: Learning from renowned figures and their Enneagram types.
- **Chapter 6 - Meet Your Purpose**: Discovering how your personality guides your life purpose.
- **Chapter 7 - Meet Your Tool for Better Mental Health**: Exploring how personality health impacts mental and emotional well-being.
- **Chapter 8 - Meet the New YOU 2.0**: Embrace your transformation and step into a more empowered, self-aware version of yourself.

Each chapter will introduce you to a new aspect of Personality Awareness, deepening your understanding of yourself and others, and giving you practical tools you can apply immediately.

Your Journey Begins Here

Personality Awareness isn't just about understanding who you are—it's about harnessing that knowledge to create a better life. By the end of this book, you'll have insights that can transform your relationships, improve your emotional health, and give you a greater sense of purpose. I invite you to join me on this journey, to discover the excitement and potential of Personality Awareness, and to start living with more intention and connection every day.

Chapter 1: Meet Your Autopilot

Understanding the Subconscious and Conscious Mind

Imagine a tool so powerful it could unlock a new level of self-awareness and understanding, one that reveals the intricate connections between who you are and how you see others. *Personality Awareness* is that tool—a gateway to truly understanding the automatic responses and ingrained patterns that shape our interactions, perceptions, and emotions. It's a journey into the subconscious, our "autopilot," a part of us that operates silently yet constantly, guiding us based on past experiences, beliefs, and instincts.

Our subconscious is at work every moment, shaping decisions, influencing emotions, and impacting how we connect with others. Without realizing it, we live much of our lives on autopilot, driven by automatic responses that often feel beyond our control. But what if you could bring that hidden part of yourself into the light, gaining the ability to understand, guide, and even transform it? Personality Awareness is your guide on this journey. It begins with understanding the subconscious—your autopilot—and learning to partner it with your conscious mind to create a more intentional, purpose-driven life.

The Subconscious: Your Hidden Autopilot

Have you ever met someone and felt an immediate, unexplainable impression—maybe a strong sense of trust or a vague discomfort? Perhaps as you reflected on that first meeting, you found reasons to explain your instinct, noticing the way they stood, their tone of voice, or a particular expression. That initial feeling was your subconscious autopilot at work, responding with automatic, deeply ingrained perceptions based on past experiences and internal patterns. It spoke before your conscious mind even had the chance to analyze.

The subconscious is like the vast body of an iceberg beneath the surface, powerful and unseen. It holds your instincts, emotional responses, and automatic behaviors—the habits that you've formed, the experiences you've internalized, the motivations that steer your decisions. When you walk into a room and immediately sense whether you feel comfortable or on edge, it's your subconscious making a snap judgment, swiftly and without conscious thought.

Our autopilot doesn't need to "think" because it already knows, drawn from a reservoir of past experiences. This is what we sometimes call "gut feeling" or "intuition"—a response that comes from deep within, often without explanation.

It's also this part of our mind that drives emotional responses, which can sometimes be mysterious. Have you ever walked away from a conversation feeling uneasy but couldn't pinpoint why? That's the autopilot again, reacting instinctively, sometimes faster than the conscious mind can interpret. The subconscious serves as a protector, an influencer, a guide that shapes how you experience the world without needing you to direct it consciously. In many ways, it's our first reaction, constantly "on" in the background, ready to act.

The Conscious Mind: The Voice of Intention

While the subconscious operates automatically, the conscious mind is slower, intentional, and deliberate. It's the voice you hear in your head—the part of you that makes plans, thinks critically, and rationalizes. Your conscious mind steps in after the subconscious has made its automatic decision, and it attempts to make sense of what's happened. This is why, after a first impression, your conscious mind might go to work looking for reasons: *Why do I feel so drawn to this person?* or *What about them made me uncomfortable?*

Imagine you're at a gathering, and you suddenly feel uneasy around someone. Your subconscious has already responded with its swift judgment based on subtle cues—body language, a tone of voice, perhaps something familiar yet unidentifiable. Then, the conscious mind steps in, questioning, reasoning, and reflecting: *Was it something they said?* or *Did they remind me of someone?*

Your conscious mind is the space where self-awareness grows. It allows you to reflect on your actions, decisions, and even your automatic responses, considering whether they align with your values and intentions. In this way, the conscious mind is our navigator, working with the subconscious to shape a purposeful life.

The Interplay Between Subconscious and Conscious

Though they serve different roles, the subconscious and conscious minds work together to shape who we are. The subconscious is quick, reactive, emotional, and automatic—an autopilot shaped by experiences, instincts, and habits. The conscious mind, on the other hand, is slower, more analytical, and focused on reflection and reasoning.

This interplay is the key to understanding our personality. Much of what drives us comes from the subconscious—our deeply ingrained patterns of thought and emotional responses. Yet, it's through the conscious mind, the voice of intention, that we can become aware of these patterns and begin to shape our lives in new directions.

Understanding this balance is where Personality Awareness begins. By recognizing and understanding how our autopilot influences us, we can begin to shape our responses and actions. We can make conscious choices that align more deeply with who we truly are and want to be.

The Story of You: The Beginning of Personality Awareness

This journey of Personality Awareness begins with understanding these two powerful systems working in tandem. The more you pay attention to your subconscious autopilot—how it subtly influences your feelings and reactions—the more clarity you gain on your deeper motivations and patterns. This awareness opens the door to self-understanding and growth, where you can start noticing automatic responses, gut reactions, and the logical justifications that follow.

By cultivating this awareness, you don't turn off your autopilot; instead, you learn to partner with it, gaining the ability to direct it with intention. This is the start of greater self-awareness, one where you're not only more intentional in your actions but also more empathetic and perceptive toward others.

Embracing Your Autopilot: The Power of Personality Awareness

Imagine having the tools to understand your automatic responses, those snap judgments and emotional reactions that seem to spring out of nowhere. This is what Personality Awareness offers: a path to seeing how our subconscious autopilot shapes our lives, often without us realizing it. By learning to identify and regulate this autopilot, we gain a blueprint for living with purpose, improving self-awareness, and deepening our understanding of others.

As you've read, our subconscious is like a silent autopilot, navigating our daily interactions and emotions based on stored experiences and instinctual responses. Yet this autopilot doesn't have to run unchecked. Personality Awareness is one of the most advanced ways to truly understand our inner mechanisms, enabling us to consciously guide our actions rather than react purely out of habit or past conditioning.

Through this awareness, you're stepping into a new dimension of understanding—one where your life can be directed with intention and clarity, where you're not only seeing yourself but also seeing others with greater compassion and purpose. This chapter is just the beginning of a journey that will help you master your autopilot and use it to enhance every part of your life.

Chapter 2: Meet The Enneagram

The Enneagram and My Journey of Discovery

In the pursuit of understanding my subconscious autopilot, I explored nearly every personality system available. From Myers-Briggs to DISC to the Four Temperaments, each offered unique insights, but nothing resonated as deeply as the Enneagram. It was the Enneagram that truly illuminated the layers of my personality and brought clarity to my interactions with others. It didn't just reveal aspects of who I am; it offered a transformative perspective that bridged the gap between my subconscious and conscious mind.

My wife first introduced me to the Enneagram during the early years of our marriage. Despite counseling and numerous attempts to resolve differences, we often found ourselves at an impasse—two strong-willed individuals struggling to understand each other. But learning about the Enneagram became a turning point. We weren't just seeing each other through assumptions or past patterns; we were seeing each other with a new depth and compassion. The Enneagram had given us a shared language, revealing not only the traits we held but the motivations beneath them. In understanding each other's personality types, we learned to dismantle misinterpretations and bring a deeper harmony to our marriage.

This was more than self-discovery; it was relationship-saving. The Enneagram showed me that it is possible to live in sync with those around us by honoring each other's unique patterns. With this profound experience, I became eager to explore it further and to apply its lessons in all areas of my life.

Why the Enneagram? Identifying and Regulating Your Autopilot

What sets the Enneagram apart is its power to pinpoint our automatic tendencies—our autopilot responses that often run beneath conscious awareness. It reveals not just what we do but why we do it, making it the ultimate tool for identifying and regulating our subconscious motives. When we experience intense emotions like guilt, fear, or anger without understanding their root, the Enneagram helps us trace these back to core fears, desires, and patterns. It's as if the Enneagram shines a light on the inner workings of our minds, exposing the autopilot settings that shape our perceptions, decisions, and reactions.

Through Personality Awareness, we use the Enneagram to uncover and regulate these automatic responses. It challenges us to confront our blind spots and to recognize when we're projecting onto others or misinterpreting their motives. The Enneagram enables us to see ourselves and others with clarity, leading to a more transparent, harmonious way of interacting. By learning to identify and adjust our subconscious patterns, we unlock new ways of responding—ultimately improving our relationships and self-understanding.

Making Personality Awareness Practical: Applying the Enneagram to Everyday Life

The beauty of the Enneagram lies in its practicality. Rather than just offering labels or categories, it provides a map for daily interactions, a guide to better understanding yourself and others in real-time. With each interaction, each decision, and each moment of introspection, the Enneagram gives us an opportunity to bring awareness to our actions and to intentionally shape our responses.

In my own life, Personality Awareness transformed everyday conversations. Where I once felt frustration, I found empathy. Where I might have judged, I became curious. Learning to apply the Enneagram practically has changed my relationships from surface-level exchanges to deeper, more meaningful connections. With every new insight into my own type—and the types of those around me—I saw an opportunity for growth, patience, and compassion.

Imagine knowing that someone you love struggles with self-doubt or thrives on affirmation because of their Enneagram type. Rather than interpreting their reactions personally, you begin to understand them in the context of their unique patterns. This understanding doesn't just help you; it empowers them to feel seen and supported. The Enneagram becomes a language of connection, providing insights that transcend surface differences and foster lasting bonds.

Cultivating Patience and Compassion through the Enneagram

One of the greatest gifts of Personality Awareness through the Enneagram is the patience and compassion it cultivates. Knowing someone's Enneagram type helps us anticipate their responses and view them through a lens of understanding rather than judgment. For instance, learning that my wife and I approach challenges from different perspectives allowed me to stop taking her reactions personally. Rather than frustration, I found myself developing a sense of empathy that deepened our bond.

When we understand each other's Enneagram types, we stop seeing actions as mere annoyances or quirks. We recognize the motivations and needs beneath them. This understanding allows us to support each other in ways that truly resonate, ultimately enhancing patience, compassion, and emotional intimacy.

Beyond Ourselves: How Personality Awareness Transforms All Relationships

The insights I gained from the Enneagram didn't stay within my immediate relationships. As I began sharing these principles with friends, colleagues, and other couples, I witnessed a profound ripple effect. Couples found themselves appreciating each other's differences, and friendships deepened as people learned to honor each other's unique perspectives. The Enneagram helped people articulate emotions they had long felt but never fully understood, allowing them to connect with loved ones on a more genuine level.

In every case, Personality Awareness brought a newfound respect for the individuality of others. It's not about trying to fit everyone into a mold; it's about embracing diversity in a way that strengthens connection. When we view others through the lens of the Enneagram, we move from mere tolerance to appreciation, from frustration to compassion. The Enneagram invites us to meet others where they are and celebrate them as they are.

Personality Awareness: The Art of Interpreting the Mind Through the Enneagram

Personality Awareness is the art of interpreting both the conscious and subconscious mind through the lens of the Enneagram. It goes beyond self-discovery, empowering us to understand the full spectrum of motivations, instincts, and logical processes that shape who we are. By understanding our own Enneagram type, we learn the art of self-awareness. By learning about others 'types, we gain the ability to create harmony in our relationships.

The Enneagram serves as a roadmap for interpreting the internal forces that drive our decisions. Through its insights, we begin to see patterns that were once invisible, tracing automatic behaviors back to their roots and cultivating conscious responses that better align with our goals and values.

Your First Step: Discovering Your Enneagram Type

Before we explore all nine Enneagram types in detail, the most important step is learning your own. This discovery marks the beginning of your journey into Personality Awareness. When you understand your own type, you gain insight into patterns you may never have fully recognized. You begin to see why you react a certain way under stress, why certain decisions resonate with you, and why you connect with some people more naturally than others.

This knowledge isn't just enlightening—it's transformative. As you embrace your Enneagram type, you will start to observe your subconscious patterns in action, giving you the power to respond intentionally rather than react automatically. This heightened self-awareness is not only a pathway to personal growth but also a foundation for building empathy and understanding with others.

Conclusion: Embracing the Journey of Personality Awareness

As you dive into the world of Personality Awareness, you're embarking on a journey that will elevate your self-awareness, transform your relationships, and offer a blueprint for understanding yourself and others with purpose. Through the Enneagram, you'll learn to identify your autopilot responses and to choose, with intention, responses that align with your values and your vision for the person you want to become.

The Enneagram is more than a tool—it's a key to unlocking the highest potential within yourself and within those around you. Let this journey inspire you to embrace the full depth of your personality, to connect with others in new ways, and to live each day with a renewed sense of purpose and clarity. In doing so, you'll find that Personality Awareness isn't just a study; it's a way of life. And it starts now, with you.

Chapter 3: Meet Your Inner Counsel – The Heart, Head, and Body, our Centers of Intelligence

Introduction: The Power of Inner Counsel

In every decision we make, whether big or small, there are forces at play that we may not fully understand. We often rely on "autopilot" responses driven by ingrained patterns. According to the Enneagram, these automatic responses can be grouped into three main decision drivers—our intellect, emotions, and instincts. These three, in combination, drive our decisions because they are the way our inner intelligence communicates. Our inner intelligence is known as our three Centers of Intelligence- The Head (intellect), The Heart (emotions), and The Body (instincts). Together, these make up what we can think of as our inner counsel, a board of directors within us that shapes how we perceive the world and respond to it.

In this chapter, we'll explore how each part of our inner counsel—the Head, Heart, and Body Centers of Intelligence —can serve as guides. By tapping into these inner voices, we gain a deeper understanding of ourselves and bring a practical awareness to our everyday lives. This is the essence of *Personality Awareness*—using the Enneagram Center of Intelligence to elevate self-awareness to new dimensions.

Introducing Your Inner Counsel: Head, Heart, and Body

Imagine these three Centers of Intelligence as board members within your mind, each contributing a unique perspective to the decisions you make:

- **The Head (Logic)** – Representing intellect, this inner advisor is driven by reason and logic, carefully weighing pros and cons and striving for security and clarity.
- **The Heart (Emotions)** – Embracing emotions, this counselor draws on empathy and emotional connection, guiding decisions based on feelings and intuitions.
- **The Body (Instincts)** – This guide operates on instincts, acting quickly and decisively based on what feels right or safe in the moment, with a strong focus on instinctual needs.

Much like consulting a diverse board of advisors, tuning into these aspects of ourselves creates a balanced perspective. Through *Personality Awareness*, we can engage each voice deliberately by listening to our inner dialogue, gaining a better understanding of our underlying motivations and learning how to make decisions that align with our true values.

How Each Center of Intelligence Guides Us in Everyday Decisions

To understand how these three guides operate in daily life, imagine a simple choice—what to eat:

- **Head (Logic)** – You find yourself choosing a healthy option, reasoning through the dietary benefits, and aligning with long-term health goals. This approach is rational and driven by logical thought, characteristic of the Head Center of Intelligence.
- **Heart (Emotions)** – You go for a slice of cake, choosing it because it reminds you of joyful celebrations with loved ones. Here, the Heart Center of Intelligence influence is felt, as emotions guide your choices.
- **Body (Instincts)** – You grab a quick, convenient snack, reacting to your hunger without overthinking. This choice is immediate and instinctual, driven by the Body's Center of Intelligence focus on survival and satisfaction.

Each Center of Intelligence represents a distinct, natural way of approaching life. Recognizing how they influence us in these small, everyday decisions helps us see how powerful they are in guiding our more complex choices.

Connecting the Centers of Intelligence to the Conscious and Subconscious Mind

Each Center of Intelligence not only shapes our decisions but operates at different levels within our mind, both consciously and subconsciously. The Head often engages the conscious mind, while the Heart and Body often tap into the subconscious, where patterns, reflexes, and intuition live.

Imagine your mind as a computer with two processors:

- **The Conscious Processor** – This processor is slow but deliberate, turning on when you actively problem-solve or make considered choices.
- **The Subconscious Processor** – This processor is fast and always running, taking over for our habitual and emotional responses.

Understanding these two parts of our mind helps us recognize when a decision is influenced by conscious thought or subconscious habit, allowing us to interact more fully with each Center of Intelligence. By understanding which Center of Intelligence speaks up and how, we gain insight into whether our response is intentional or automatic, and we can adjust accordingly.

Embracing the Centers of Intelligence in Everyday Life

One of the practical benefits of *Personality Awareness* is learning how to make these inner voices work together as we navigate life. When we acknowledge each Center of Intelligence's insights and recognize their unique contributions, we become more balanced decision-makers and develop a deeper understanding of ourselves.

Consider these approaches to make each Center of Intelligence influence practical in daily life:

- **Listen to the Inner Dialogue of Our Body (instinctual intelligence)** – When we tune into our body's instincts, we become more in tune with our basic needs and physical boundaries, helping us manage our energy, safety, and well-being. There are some practical self-care inclinations that our body gives us. Like drinking more water, exercising, sleeping, and stretching, to name a few. If we eat something unhealthy and feel bad, our body will take note and warn us for next time. It's up to us to listen to our body and it will let us know how to take care of it.

- **Listen to the Inner Dialogue of Our Heart (emotional intelligence)** – By tuning into our heart, we build stronger connections with others, allowing emotional intelligence to guide us in relational decisions and helping us to align with our core values. The areas where I see we need the most help to listen to our heart is how we treat others with value and care. If we tap into the emotional capacity of our heart when dealing with others, it will help us imagine how another person would feel. So, the golden rule of treating others how you would treat yourself is learned by using our Heart Center of Intelligence. And some of us do have a hard time thinking with our feelings when dealing with others, but that mindset is the essence of emotional intelligence: being able to read the room and image how others feel by looking at their body language and facial expressions. And then listening to your heart to treat them how they want to be treated.

- **Listen to the Inner Dialogue of Our Head (intellectual intelligence)** – Engaging our head helps us access reason and rationality, supporting clearer thinking, planning, and creating pathways for long-term success. My tip for people who are emotionally driven is to listen to your head more. When my wife tells me about a situation and gives me an emotional perspective, I ask her, "what does your head say?" This helps her switch the sound track inside her mind to another perspective that she already has in her inner counsel. And she would articulate to me a rational response to the emotional situation. This shows she already has access to her head's Center of Intelligence rationale, but she has to turn off her emotional autopilot to listen to her logical inner voice.

When we start using these voices intentionally, we have the power to make informed choices that reflect our true selves, rather than letting our autopilot responses steer us.

Why the Enneagram Separates Personality Types by Their Center of Intelligence (AKA The Three Triads)

The Enneagram simplifies our understanding of personality types by organizing the nine types into three triads, each guided by a core decision driver as our main Center of Intelligence. Normally, we use all three Centers of Intelligence in combination, but one usually dominates, shaping how we approach challenges, relationships, and growth.

The Triad Centers of Intelligence are as follows:

- **Head Triad (Types 5, 6, 7)** – Guided by intellect and logic, these individuals are thinkers. Often motivated by a need for security, they process decisions mentally and analyze situations carefully.
- **Heart Triad (Types 2, 3, 4)** – Driven by emotions and intuition, these individuals are feelers. Seeking connection and approval, they rely on empathy and intuition to guide them through choices and interactions.
- **Body Triad (Types 8, 9, 1)** – Led by instincts, these types respond quickly and instinctively to situations. With a focus on autonomy, they rely on gut feelings and a desire for control.

By focusing on triads rather than individual types, we can begin to understand people on a more foundational level. This triadic structure offers a simpler, more accessible framework for understanding personality types and preparing us to dive deeper into each type's unique strengths, challenges, and motivations.

The Enneagram provides a blueprint for understanding our personality's autopilot. Each personality type has its default settings—patterns of thought, feeling, and action that shape how we interact with the world. These patterns are not random; they are rooted in deeply embedded guiding principles. These principles are the subconscious filters that determine how we interpret and respond to life.

Guiding Principles and the Triads

Every personality type within the Enneagram falls into one of three triads: the Head, Heart, or Body. Each triad is guided by a core principle that operates on autopilot, influencing how we process our experiences:

- **Head Triad (Types 5, 6, 7)**: Guided by true or false. Their subconscious evaluates situations through the lens of clarity and logic. This principle addresses their core need for security and certainty. They instinctively analyze situations, seeking answers and certainty to resolve some level of fear. Their thoughts guide them to evaluate what is intellectually sound or unsafe.
- **Heart Triad (Types 2, 3, 4)**: Guided by good or bad. Their subconscious seeks connection and validation, using emotional vibrations and discernment of energy to navigate relationships and self-worth. Their feelings guide them to determine what feels affirming or painful, often seeking validation and connection to resolve levels of shame.
- **Body Triad (Types 8, 9, 1)**: Guided by right or wrong. Their subconscious relies on instinct and integrity, responding to life with a visceral sense of justice and action. Their gut reactions guide them toward what feels just or unjust, often driven by an unconscious desire to resolve some levels of anger.

Each guiding principle is like a compass, silently directing the course of our thoughts, emotions, and decisions.

An Illustration of Guiding Principles

Imagine three friends—Noah, Emma, and Claire—encountering a small, injured dog by the side of the road. Each responds instinctively, their guiding principle shaping their reaction.

- Noah, from the Head Triad, searches for facts. He needs to understand the situation before acting, asking questions like, *How serious is the injury? What's the safest solution?* His guiding principle of *true or false* drives him to analyze first.

- Emma, from the Heart Triad, immediately feels the dog's pain. She reaches out with empathy, wanting to soothe its suffering, guided by her principle of *good or bad*.

- Claire, from the Body Triad, acts decisively. Her sense of *right or wrong* compels her to take charge, ensuring the dog gets help. She doesn't need all the answers or to process her feelings—she instinctively knows the just thing to do.

This story shows how our guiding principles shape our subconscious autopilot. Each triad's guiding principle operates automatically, influencing how we respond to the world and the challenges we face. Each friend's subconscious *autopilot* led them to respond in their own way—through thought, feeling, or instinct. Their guiding principles shaped their actions, highlighting the strengths and limitations of their unique approaches.

And the life skill we can get from Personality Awareness is to respect the different perspectives each triad is guided by. Knowing that some people move faster than others. And some personalities are slower to process. And others have a harder time showing emotions. We all should accept that each personality type has an inherent advantage in some arenas and given a chance, any personality can adapt to get the job done in many different aspects in life.

Connecting Subconscious and Conscious Awareness

While we are each primarily guided by one guiding principle, Personality Awareness allows us to recognize and engage with our other inner guidance. Think of it as an inner council of voices: thought, feeling, and instinct. Depending on your Enneagram type, one voice will naturally take the lead on autopilot, but the others are always present, waiting to be heard.

For example:

- A Type 6 (Head Triad) may naturally analyze everything for security but can benefit from tuning into their emotions or instincts when overthinking becomes paralyzing.

- A Type 3 (Heart Triad) may instinctively seek validation but can gain clarity by asking logical questions or grounding themselves in their values.

- A Type 8 (Body Triad) may rely on their gut instincts but find balance by considering facts or exploring how their actions affect others emotionally.

The goal is not to silence your primary guiding principle but to expand your awareness to include all three. This integration moves you from being controlled by your autopilot to consciously navigating your life with wisdom and balance.

In the next chapter, we'll explore these nine Enneagram types individually, gaining insight into how each one expresses its core triad traits.

Conclusion: Embracing the Journey of Personality Awareness

Personality awareness is a journey of discovering the layers within us, a practice of observing our head, heart, and body voices and learning to harmonize them. Each Center of Intelligence offers invaluable wisdom when we tune into it with intention. Imagine a life where your choices aren't made on autopilot but are conscious decisions, guided by a deep understanding of who you are.

Through the art of Personality Awareness, you'll learn to recognize and honor each part of yourself, bringing clarity and purpose to your actions. Embracing this journey means stepping into a new level of self-awareness, where your choices reflect the full breadth of your unique personality. As you continue to grow in understanding, you'll find a profound freedom in knowing yourself deeply, navigating life with a balanced inner counsel, and seeing the world with new eyes.

Chapter 4: Meet Your Personality

Introduction: The Art of Self-Knowledge

Knowing ourselves deeply is both an art and a skill. Imagine a sculptor refining each stroke to reveal the figure hidden within the marble. Similarly, Personality Awareness provides us with tools to uncover and understand the motivations, strengths, and blind spots that shape who we are.

In this chapter, we'll explore how the Enneagram is more than a personality classification; it's a framework that empowers us to know ourselves in transformative ways. By discovering our Enneagram type, we take the first steps toward what I call "Full Personality Awareness"—a state where we see ourselves clearly, make intentional choices, and navigate life with deeper self-awareness.

Discovering Your Enneagram Type

Your journey to self-discovery begins by exploring the nine types within the Enneagram. The Enneagram is like a mirror, showing us aspects of ourselves we may not have seen clearly before. As you learn about your type, you'll uncover core motivations that have influenced you throughout your life (aka your subconscious autopilot). The insights you gain here can be used to level up your self-awareness, allowing you to approach life with greater clarity and purpose.

Introduction and Overview of the Nine Enneagram Types

The Enneagram introduces us to nine distinct personality types, each shaped by a unique way of perceiving the world, making decisions, and managing emotions. These types are organized into three triads—the Heart, Head, and Body triads—based on their center of intelligence.

Each triad has a dominant emotion: shame, fear, or anger. These emotions influence their behavior and can trigger subconsciously, which is why I refer to them as the "autopilot" emotions. Without intentional effort, these autopilot emotions guide our decisions in ways we may not fully realize. By understanding the automatic emotional responses of each type, we gain insight into not only our own tendencies but also the emotional experiences of those around us.

This introduction to the nine types is more than classification—it's a journey into emotional intelligence. As we explore each type, we begin to understand the emotions that drive them. This awareness equips us to recognize and empathize with others 'feelings, fostering deeper and more meaningful relationships.

Meet the Nine Types:

Type 1 – The Reformer (Body Triad)

Driven by a strong sense of right and wrong, Reformers are principled, idealistic, and determined to make the world better. They live with a constant inner critic, urging them to strive for perfection, yet they often wrestle with anger, which they suppress as frustration when things fall short of their standards.

Imagine a meticulous structural engineer designing a masterpiece, feeling both inspired by their vision and burdened by every tiny flaw they see. Reformers tend to see the world as a place that needs improvement, where their role is to restore order and integrity in the face of imperfection.

Type 2 – The Helper (Heart Triad)

The Helper's world revolves around love and connection. Generous and warm, they find fulfillment in caring for others, often putting others 'needs before their own. However, Helpers battle shame, feeling unworthy unless they are constantly giving.

Picture a gardener tending to a vibrant garden—not for themselves, but to brighten the lives of those who walk through it. Helpers often view the world through the lens of relationships, believing their worth is tied to how much they contribute to others 'happiness.

Type 3 – The Achiever (Heart Triad)

Achievers are driven by success and recognition. Charismatic and adaptable, they work tirelessly to excel in whatever they pursue. Beneath their confident exterior, however, lies the shame of falling short of expectations, both their own and others'.

Think of a star athlete crossing the finish line, exhilarated by victory but haunted by the pressure to maintain their title. Achievers see the world as a stage where their accomplishments determine their value and strive to perform flawlessly to earn admiration.

Type 4 – The Individualist (Heart Triad)

Deeply introspective and creative, Individualists are on a quest for authenticity and meaning. They long to feel special and unique but often wrestle with feelings of shame, fearing they'll never truly belong.

Picture a poet pouring their soul onto a page, capturing beauty in their pain. Individualists tend to see the world as a canvas for self-expression, where their value lies in being distinct and deeply understood.

Type 5 – The Investigator (Head Triad)

Investigators are curious, analytical, and independent. They crave knowledge as a way to feel secure in an unpredictable world. Beneath their quest for understanding lies a core fear of being unprepared or overwhelmed.

Imagine a scholar surrounded by books, seeking answers to life's mysteries in solitude. Investigators often see the world as a complex puzzle, believing that mastery of information will provide safety and clarity in uncertain circumstances.

Type 6 – The Loyalist (Head Triad)

The Loyalist is a steady, reliable presence in any group. They're deeply motivated by security and trust, often scanning their environment for potential threats. Their dominant emotion is fear, which fuels their vigilance but can also lead to doubt and anxiety.

Picture an air traffic controller tirelessly watching the horizon for signs of danger to protect the planes in the area. Loyalists see the world as unpredictable and often feel it's their responsibility to anticipate risks and protect the people and systems they trust.

Type 7 – The Enthusiast (Head Triad)

Enthusiasts radiate energy and optimism, seeking freedom and joy in every experience. Beneath their love of adventure, however, lies a fear of pain or being trapped in discomfort, driving them to keep moving.

Imagine a world traveler with an ever-growing list of destinations, always seeking the next thrill. Enthusiasts often see the world as a playground of opportunities, where their goal is to avoid limitations and pursue endless excitement.

Type 8 – The Challenger (Body Triad)

Bold and protective, Challengers value control and autonomy. They exude strength and confidence, often stepping in to shield the vulnerable. Yet, their underlying emotion is anger, which they channel into asserting themselves and avoiding vulnerability.

Picture a warrior standing guard at the gates, fiercely defending what they hold dear. Challengers view the world as a place that demands strength and resilience, where survival depends on asserting their power and protecting what matters most.

Type 9 – The Peacemaker (Body Triad)

Peacemakers are calm, accepting, and driven by a desire for harmony and unity. They strive to avoid conflict at all costs, often suppressing their own needs to maintain peace. Their repressed anger can quietly build until it surfaces unexpectedly.

Imagine a mediator smoothing tensions between opposing sides, their presence like a gentle breeze on a turbulent day. Peacemakers see the world as a space that thrives on unity and balance, often believing that their role is to preserve harmony at the expense of their own desires.

Why the Nine Types Matter

These nine types represent the diverse ways we perceive, react, and connect with the world. Each type has its own challenges and strengths, offering us different views of the human experience.

By learning these types, we gain more than self-awareness—we cultivate emotional intelligence. We begin to see why others feel and act as they do, unlocking the potential for deeper empathy and understanding. This is the foundation of Personality Awareness: recognizing and appreciating the unique design of every individual, and using that knowledge to navigate relationships and life with intention.

Core Drives and the Motive of Personalities

Now that we've introduced the nine personality types, let's uncover what truly drives each of them. Every personality type isn't just about what we do—it's about why we do it. The secret lies in our **core drive**—the invisible fuel powering our subconscious autopilot.

These core drives are the hidden motives that shape our behavior, emotions, and relationships. They're like the software running in the background, influencing every decision we make. And here's the exciting part: **Personality Awareness** gives us the tools to decode these core drives—not just in ourselves, but in others, too.

Imagine reading the room, and you can discern not just what someone is doing, but what's propelling them forward beneath the surface. That's the level of insight **Personality Awareness** offers—a step beyond any other personality system. It's the key to understanding why people think, feel, and act the way they do.

The Three Triads and Their Core Drives:

At the heart of every personality type lies a **core drive**, a compelling motive deeply rooted in our subconscious autopilot. These motives define how we respond to the world, but more importantly, they reveal what we're searching for in life.

Heart Triad (Types 2, 3, 4):

These personalities are driven by a need to find **identity and significance**. Deep down, their autopilot is navigating the emotional waters of connection and worth.

- **Core Drive**: The need to create or sustain a sense of identity and significance.
- **Autopilot Desire**: These types are motivated by the desire to feel loved, valued, and recognized for who they are.

Autopilot Emotion: The core emotion driving the subconscious is shame, which manifests in various forms, including feelings of guilt, embarrassment, inadequacy, self-doubt, depression, and a general sense of feeling bad. These variations reveal the spectrum of emotions the Heart Triad can experience on autopilot, particularly in response to stress.

- **Type 2**: Strives to earn love by being helpful and indispensable.
- **Type 3**: Seeks admiration through achievement and success.
- **Type 4**: Aims to create significance through authenticity and uniqueness.

Head Triad (Types 5, 6, 7):

These types are motivated by a need for **security and stability**. Beneath the surface, their autopilot is working to outmaneuver fear and uncertainty.

- **Core Drive**: The need for security and stability.
- **Autopilot Desire**: These types are motivated by the desire to overcome fear and anxiety by seeking clarity, guidance, or experiences that minimize uncertainty.

Autopilot Emotion: The core emotion driving the subconscious is fear, which manifests in various forms, including nervousness, concern, caution, worry, unease, insecurity, paranoia, and anxiety. These variations reveal the spectrum of emotions the Head Triad can experience on autopilot, particularly in response to stress.

- **Type 5**: Seeks security through knowledge and understanding.
- **Type 6**: Looks for safety through loyalty and preparedness.
- **Type 7**: Avoids fear by seeking pleasure and avoiding pain or limitations.

Gut Triad (Types 8, 9, 1):

For these types, the core drive is a need for **autonomy and control**. Their subconscious is tuned to issues of power, harmony, or integrity.

Core Drive: The need to assert autonomy and control their environment.

Autopilot Desire: These types are motivated by a desire to address inner conflict and external challenges. Their core emotional response is **anger**, though it manifests differently across the types.

Autopilot Emotion: The core emotion driving the subconscious is anger, which manifests in various forms, including frustration, irritation, annoyance, agitation, rage, bitterness, repressed anger, and self-directed anger. These variations reveal the spectrum of emotions the Body Triad can experience on autopilot, particularly in response to stress.

- **Type 8:** Manages anger by asserting strength and control.
- **Type 9:** Avoids anger by seeking harmony and peace.
- **Type 1:** Channels anger into striving for perfection and integrity.

Why Personality Awareness is the Ultimate Tool

Here's the game-changer: No other personality system goes as deep as **Personality Awareness** in helping us decode these subconscious motives. While other systems stop at the surface—giving you labels or traits—**Personality Awareness** dives into the autopilot steering our lives.

When you understand the core drives and autopilot systems, you're not just seeing what someone does; you're uncovering the "why" behind it—a thrilling discovery that reveals the hidden script guiding our lives. That's why Personality Awareness is the best-kept secret about ourselves. It uncovers the exciting mystery of our subconscious—a part of us most people never notice because they aren't awake to its influence.

What Personality Awareness does is use the Enneagram not just as a source of information but as a practical tool to unveil the subconscious programs I call our autopilot. By giving our subconscious a voice, name, and description, we uncover the mysterious forces operating behind the scenes. This insight transforms how we understand ourselves and others, paving the way for deeper connections, conflict resolution, and personal growth.

The Power of Knowing Yourself Deeply

Once we know our type, we can begin to see patterns in our thoughts, behaviors, and emotions. This deeper self-knowledge empowers us to make choices from a place of awareness, rather than automatic reaction. For example:

- **Type 1s** can work to release frustration by acknowledging that imperfection is part of life, rather than expecting themselves or others to always meet an ideal.

- **Type 4s** can guard against feelings of inadequacy by recognizing that they are valuable even if they don't feel "special" in every moment.

- **Type 7s** can begin to accept discomfort as a necessary part of growth, rather than avoiding it through constant activity.

When we approach our lives with awareness, we're no longer trapped by our habitual reactions. Instead, we're free to make choices that align with our values and goals. Knowing ourselves deeply is a powerful tool for change.

Practical Applications of Personality Awareness

With Personality Awareness, the Enneagram becomes a practical tool for daily life. Here's how each type might use their insights:

- **Communication**: Understanding your Enneagram type can improve how you relate to others. A Type 2, for example, can recognize when they're overextending to help others and set healthy boundaries.

- **Stress Management**: A Type 6 can notice when they're overthinking and redirect their focus toward tangible solutions.

- **Decision-Making**: A Type 5 might catch themselves analyzing a decision excessively and remind themselves to take action, even if they don't feel 100% prepared.

In each case, self-awareness allows us to respond rather than react, cultivating healthier habits in our relationships, careers, and personal lives.

Conclusion: Your Path to Full Personality Awareness

Self-discovery through the Enneagram is a journey, not a destination. Knowing your type isn't just an end goal; it's the beginning of a path to greater self-understanding. As you learn to use Personality Awareness, you'll not only enhance your own life but gain tools that benefit all your relationships and experiences.

This journey to full Personality Awareness empowers you to live with greater clarity, purpose, and fulfillment. By knowing yourself deeply, you'll find that the insights you gain here are the foundation for a life of intentionality, resilience, and meaningful connections.

Chapter 5: Meet Famous Enneagram Personalities from History

Introduction

Personality types are more than abstract ideas; they're a blueprint for understanding how we—and those around us—shape our world. By looking at lives that exemplify each Enneagram type, we see how our personality in action can leave a lasting impact. These stories allow us to recognize similar traits in those around us and inspire us to treat others as they truly wish to be treated. Personality Awareness becomes the art of truly perceiving others—understanding their motivations and responding with empathy and wisdom.

This chapter will introduce each Enneagram type through a historical figure's story, capturing the thoughts, emotions, and motivations that define each personality. Let's look deeper into these remarkable lives to find clues about recognizing and connecting with the people in our own lives.

Type 1 - The Reformer

Martin Luther King Jr.

Martin Luther King Jr. was a visionary and reformer whose life was defined by an unshakable commitment to justice, equality, and nonviolent resistance. Growing up in the segregated American South, King witnessed the brutal injustices of racial discrimination. But instead of accepting this harsh reality, he believed in a higher moral standard and a world in which all people could be free and equal. He dedicated his life to this ideal, leading a movement that would change the course of history. Even in the face of violence, hatred, and imprisonment, King remained steadfast in his principles, challenging society to rise to a higher moral ground. His pursuit of justice was rooted in a deep personal integrity—King held himself accountable to the same standards of love, courage, and fairness that he preached, embodying the change he wished to see in the world.

- **Quote:** "Injustice anywhere is a threat to justice everywhere."

- **Common Thoughts for This Personality Type:** "What is morally right in this situation?" "How can I fight for justice?" "There is a higher ideal that we must all strive for."

- **Recognizable Traits That Exemplify Type 1:** A powerful commitment to moral integrity, an unwavering sense of justice, and an inspiring vision for a fairer and more compassionate world.

Type 2 - The Helper

Mother Teresa

For Mother Teresa, compassion wasn't a lofty idea; it was the very breath of her life. She served the forgotten and impoverished in the slums of Calcutta, finding profound meaning in every small act of kindness. Her heart was open, and her hands were never idle, caring for the sick and hungry with a quiet, powerful love. Mother Teresa believed that the world needed more small acts of great love, and she lived that belief every day, inspiring countless others to join her in service.

- **Quote**: "Not all of us can do great things. But we can do small things with great love."

- **Common Thoughts For This Personality Type**: "How can I help?" "I'm needed here." "I find meaning in caring for others."

- **Recognizable Traits That Exemplify Type 2**: A deep commitment to others' well-being, an instinct to help in practical ways, and a profound belief in the power of love to heal.

Type 3 - The Achiever

Alexander Hamilton

Hamilton's life was defined by his drive to rise above his circumstances and leave an indelible mark. Born out of wedlock and raised in poverty, he climbed the ranks to become one of America's Founding Fathers. Driven by a fierce ambition and an unyielding work ethic, Hamilton saw opportunity everywhere and pursued it with unmatched vigor. Though his relentless push for success sometimes isolated him, his achievements and legacy remain. His story reflects a deep hunger to succeed and an unshakable belief in his own potential.

- **Quote:** " I am not throwing away my shot."

- **Common Thoughts For This Personality Type:** " I have to succeed." "What's my next goal?" "How will this reflect on me?"

- **Recognizable Traits That Exemplify Type 3**: A strong desire for recognition, high-performance mindset, and an intense drive to achieve.

Type 4 - The Individualist

Frida Kahlo

Frida Kahlo's life and art were one—a canvas onto which she poured her soul. Her work reveals her search for identity, a raw expression of joy, pain, love, and loss. Despite chronic illness and heartbreak, Kahlo painted her truth, capturing the beauty and complexity of her inner world. Through her self-portraits, she offered a glimpse into her emotions, her experiences, and her resilience, inviting others to find beauty in their own struggles. Frida's journey of self-discovery left behind art that still resonates deeply with those who seek to understand themselves.

- **Quote**:" I paint myself because I am so often alone and because I am the subject I know best."

- **Common Thoughts For This Personality Type**:" What is my unique contribution?" "I need to understand myself deeply." "Why do I feel different?"

- **Recognizable Traits That Exemplify Type 4**: A powerful drive for self-expression, a rich inner world, and a deep desire to understand and reveal one's true self.

Type 5 - The Investigator

Marie Curie

Marie Curie's fascination with the unknown led her into uncharted scientific territory. Her research on radioactivity required intense concentration and sacrifice, and she often worked alone, avoiding distractions to fully engage with her discoveries. Curie's devotion to knowledge, at the cost of personal health and comfort, led to breakthroughs in science that forever changed medicine. Her life reflects the Investigator's quest for understanding and independence, her unrelenting curiosity revealing the power of the human mind to push the limits of what's possible.

- **Quote**:" Nothing in life is to be feared; it is only to be understood."

- **Common Thoughts For This Personality Type**:" How does this work?" "What can I learn?" "I need time to process."

- **Recognizable Traits That Exemplify Type 5**: A passion for knowledge, preference for solitude, and an analytical approach to life.

Type 6 - The Loyalist

Oskar Schindler

Initially motivated by profit, Oskar Schindler soon found his purpose in saving lives. During World War II, he risked everything to protect his Jewish workers, showing loyalty and courage beyond what was expected. His commitment grew to a point where he would rather risk his own life than see harm come to those he considered his responsibility. Schindler's story embodies the Loyalist's deep sense of duty, the fierce attachment to those who rely on him, and the bravery to stand up for what he believed was right.

- **Quote**: "Whoever saves one life, saves the world entire."

- **Common Thoughts For This Personality Type**: "How can I keep everyone safe?" "I am responsible for those around me." "What's the best way to protect them?"

- **Recognizable Traits That Exemplify Type 6**: Fierce loyalty, a strong sense of responsibility, and a readiness to protect loved ones, especially in difficult situations.

Type 7 - The Enthusiast

Amelia Earhart

Amelia Earhart saw life as an adventure to be embraced. She flew through skies no woman had ventured before, chasing the thrill of discovery and pushing past fear. Earhart's daring spirit and love for life's possibilities made her a symbol of courage and enthusiasm. To her, every horizon held a new adventure, and every risk was a chance to grow. Her story resonates with those who see life as a boundless playground, always ready for the next thrill.

- **Quote**: "Adventure is worthwhile in itself."

- **Common Thoughts**: "What's the next big thing?" "I want to experience everything life has to offer." "How can I make this exciting?"

- **Recognizable Traits That Exemplify Type 7**: Zest for life, drive for new experiences, and an unbreakable optimism.

Type 8 - The Challenger

Harriet Tubman

Harriet Tubman's courage in leading enslaved people to freedom is the story of the Challenger in action. Tubman's strength and determination knew no bounds. She risked her life again and again to fight for justice and to protect the vulnerable. Tubman's resilience and unwavering willpower reflected her deep conviction that every person deserved freedom. Her life was a testament to the power of standing up, facing fears, and fighting for what is right.

- **Quote**: "I freed a thousand slaves. I could have freed a thousand more if only they knew they were slaves."

- **Common Thoughts For This Personality Type**: "I must be strong." "No one will control me." "What is the right battle to fight?"

- **Recognizable Traits That Exemplify Type 8**: Fearlessness, commitment to justice, and an unbreakable will.

Type 9 - The Peacemaker

Nelson Mandela

After decades of imprisonment, Nelson Mandela chose peace over revenge. He dreamed of a unified South Africa, bringing people together despite years of division. His commitment to reconciliation and understanding made him a global symbol of peace. Mandela showed that true strength lies in empathy and unity, demonstrating the power of the Peacemaker who, despite personal suffering, strives for a harmonious world.

- **Quote:**" It always seems impossible until it's done."

- **Common Thoughts For This Personality Type:**" How can I make this harmonious?" "What's the best way to create peace?" "How can I bring people together?"

- **Recognizable Traits That Exemplify Type 9**: A deep desire for unity, calm presence, and dedication to harmony.

Concluding Thoughts

These stories reveal that every personality type has something essential to offer the world. Each one plays a role that only they can fulfill, and together, they form a tapestry of diverse strengths and contributions. Embracing Personality Awareness gives us the tools to recognize these traits in those around us, helping us treat others in ways that respect their unique values and strengths. As we become more aware of these traits, we enhance our relationships, honoring the people in our lives for who they truly are.

Chapter 6: Meet Your Purpose

Introduction: Discovering the Blueprint of Your Purpose

Have you ever noticed that certain activities just light you up, while others feel like a struggle? Why do some tasks seem effortless, and others are completely draining? And why can you keep going in some areas when others have long since given up? These patterns are not coincidences; they're clues—indications of your unique purpose.

Ask yourself these questions to gain clues to your life's purpose.

1. What captures your fascination?
2. What can you accomplish effortlessly, almost without thinking?
3. What tasks can you persist with when others tire?

Your personality is like a roadmap. Within it are powerful clues about the strengths that are natural to you and the challenges you're designed to solve. By following these clues, you can meet your purpose head-on and unlock your full potential.

The Three Clues to Purpose: Fascination, Subconscious Ability, and Endurance

Purpose doesn't have to be a mystery. When you know what captivates you, where your talents flow naturally, and where you can outlast others, you begin to understand what you're truly meant to do.

1. **Fascination** — Your passions.
2. **Subconscious Ability** — Your natural gifts.
3. **Endurance** — Your ability to keep going when others can't.

Let's explore these three elements, each providing clues to help you meet your purpose.

Fascination: The Spark of Passion

Fascination is more than mere interest. It's an attraction that feels magnetic, often pulling you toward something with intensity and curiosity. True fascination draws you in, energizes you, and focuses your attention. It's a signal, pointing you to an area where your purpose might lie.

Each Enneagram triad has distinct areas of fascination:

- **Heart Triad (Types 2, 3, 4)**: Typically fascinated by people, emotions, and interpersonal connections. They are naturally drawn to understanding, helping, and inspiring others.

- **Head Triad (Types 5, 6, 7)**: Often fascinated by ideas, problem-solving, and knowledge. They're motivated by intellectual pursuits, seeking security, and exploring new possibilities.

- **Body Triad (Types 8, 9, 1)**: Typically focused on justice, control, and maintaining order. They're fascinated by real-world impact, grounded in actions, and creating stability or transformation.

Subconscious Ability: The Power of Effortless Execution

What tasks come so naturally to you that they feel effortless? Subconscious abilities represent skills that are deeply ingrained in us—so much so that we perform them without much conscious thought. These abilities reflect a core part of who we are and provide further insight into where we might find purpose.

Think of it as a "flow state," where you're able to produce excellent results without overthinking. For example, a chef might instinctively know which flavors to combine, or an artist might visualize a design with ease. This effortless execution not only points us toward areas where we're naturally skilled but also to where our purpose might lie.

Endurance: Outlasting and Excelling in Your Element

Endurance isn't just about how long you can last. True endurance is about thriving under stress, continuing forward where others would give up, and adapting to challenges that might exhaust others. It's like having an "extra gear" that engages when you're in your element, allowing you to stay committed to a task or cause long after others have faltered.

Each personality type has unique areas where they're naturally built to endure:

- **Type 1 (Reformer)**: Endures in the pursuit of improvement and justice, motivated by a desire for integrity and structure. They will keep pushing for what they believe is right, even when faced with obstacles that might dissuade others.

- **Type 2 (Helper)**: Endures in relationships, especially in providing support and care. They have a near-limitless capacity for empathy and will continue to show up for those they care about, even when others might feel drained.

- **Type 3 (Achiever)**: Endures in achieving and succeeding, driven by a desire to excel. They have a unique stamina for striving toward goals and remain focused where others might lose motivation.

- **Type 4 (Individualist)**: Endures in self-expression and creativity, often pouring themselves into their art or ideas with relentless dedication. They will explore depths of feeling and originality, long after others might shy away from the emotional intensity required.

- **Type 5 (Investigator)**: Endures in research and analysis, with a high tolerance for focus and detail. They often continue studying and exploring subjects long after others would lose interest or patience.

- **Type 6 (Loyalist)**: Endures in loyalty and vigilance, often staying committed to a cause or group despite challenges. They adapt to stress through planning and preparation, remaining steady in the face of uncertainty.

- **Type 7 (Enthusiast)**: Endures in the pursuit of new experiences and possibilities, bringing energy to areas that others might find exhausting. They push through challenges to keep exploring and experiencing life's opportunities.

- **Type 8 (Challenger)**: Endures in asserting control and pursuing justice, often thriving under pressure and confrontation. They have a drive to lead and protect, even when others might back down.

- **Type 9 (Peacemaker)**: Endures in maintaining peace and balance, patiently working through conflicts to bring harmony. They remain steadfast in their commitment to unity, enduring where others might abandon the effort for calm.

By understanding the unique ways each personality type can outlast others in their area of strength, we uncover valuable clues to purpose.

Bringing the Three Clues Together: Crafting Your Purpose Blueprint

When we combine our fascination, subconscious ability, and endurance, we create a unique map of our purpose. Each clue reveals a different aspect of where we're designed to contribute. Together, they help us pinpoint not only what we're meant to do but also how we can best achieve it.

Examples for each type help illustrate this blueprint:

Type 1 (Reformer): Fascinated by improving systems, with subconscious skills in organization, and an enduring commitment to justice. **Example**: Martin Luther King Jr., whose dedication to civil rights was driven by his relentless pursuit of equality and justice.

Type 2 (Helper): Fascinated by nurturing relationships, with a natural empathy, and enduring in providing support to others. **Example**: Princess Diana, who devoted herself to humanitarian causes and uplifted countless lives through her compassionate efforts.

Type 3 (Achiever): Fascinated by performing, with natural leadership abilities, and enduring in reaching goals. **Example**: Michael Jordan, whose dedication to winning and pushing limits made him a legend in his field.

Type 4 (Individualist): Fascinated by self-expression, with creative instincts, and enduring in artistic pursuits. **Example**: Vincent van Gogh, whose artistic passion endured despite personal struggles and challenges.

Type 5 (Investigator): Fascinated by knowledge, with analytical thinking, and enduring in the pursuit of expertise. **Example**: Albert Einstein, who tirelessly explored theories to expand our understanding of the universe.

Type 6 (Loyalist): Fascinated by safety and responsibility, with a commitment to truth, and enduring in ensuring protection for others. **Example**: Rachel Carson, whose groundbreaking work in environmental science revealed the dangers of pesticides, inspiring lasting environmental reforms.

Type 7 (Enthusiast): Fascinated by new experiences, with an adaptable spirit, and enduring in the pursuit of possibilities. **Example**: Richard Branson, whose adventurous mindset drove him to create groundbreaking companies and experiences.

Type 8 (Challenger): Fascinated by justice, with natural assertiveness, and enduring in leadership roles. **Example**: Malcolm X, whose passion for justice and resilience in advocating for human rights, shaped his legacy.

Type 9 (Peacemaker): Fascinated by unity, with subconscious patience, and enduring in conflict resolution. **Example**: Mahatma Gandhi, whose peaceful approach and endurance inspired social change.

Reflecting on Your Blueprint

Each personality type offers distinct clues to purpose. By focusing on where your fascination lies, identifying what you can accomplish without overthinking, and recognizing where you have the endurance to persist, you begin to understand your unique design.

Reflection Questions

As you ponder your personality and its connection to your purpose, consider these questions:

1. What areas of life naturally capture your fascination and make you lose track of time?
2. What subconscious strengths and instincts seem to flow effortlessly from you, even when you're unaware?
3. In what ways have you demonstrated endurance or resilience, even when faced with challenges, and how might that reveal clues to your purpose?

Take a moment to reflect on your answers. These clues provide invaluable insights into how your personality is uniquely designed to thrive. When we align our career choices with this understanding, we position ourselves to live out our purpose with fulfillment and authenticity.

Aligning Your Personality to a Dream Career

To further illuminate how our personalities guide us toward our purpose, consider how each Enneagram type might find their "dream job"—a role that resonates deeply with their core motivations and strengths:

Enneagram 1: The Reformer

- **Dream Jobs**: Judge, Non-Profit Director, Editor, Proofreader, Pilot, or Surgeon, etc
- **Why**: Reformers excel in roles that emphasize integrity, structure, and the pursuit of excellence.

Enneagram 2: The Helper

- **Dream Jobs**: Therapist, Nurse, Teacher, Mentor, or Customer Service, etc
- **Why**: Helpers thrive in positions where they can nurture, connect, and make a meaningful impact on others' lives.

Enneagram 3: The Achiever

- **Dream Jobs**: Entrepreneur, Sales Executive, Public Relations Specialist, Influencer, Podcaster, etc
- **Why**: Achievers are drawn to roles that reward ambition, offer measurable success, and provide opportunities for visibility and growth.

Enneagram 4: The Individualist

- **Dream Jobs**: Artist, Writer, Graphic Designer, Tattoo Artist, Singer, etc
- **Why**: Individualists shine in careers that allow for deep self-expression and creative exploration.

Enneagram 5: The Investigator

- **Dream Jobs**: Research Scientist, Philosopher, Engineer, Professor, Systems & Platforms Developer, Innovator, etc
- **Why**: Investigators seek intellectually stimulating environments where they can master knowledge and work independently.

Enneagram 6: The Loyalist

- **Dream Jobs**: Police Officer, Project Manager, Human Resources Specialist, Fire Marshall, Saftey Coordinator, etc

- **Why**: Loyalists thrive in structured, collaborative roles where they can create safety and stability.

Enneagram 7: The Enthusiast

- **Dream Jobs**: Travel Blogger, Event Planner, Marketing Director, DJ, Explorer, etc
- **Why**: Enthusiasts flourish in dynamic environments that offer freedom, creativity, and variety.

Enneagram 8: The Challenger

- **Dream Jobs**: CEO, Attorney, Military Officer, Entrepreneur, Builder, etc
- **Why**: Challengers excel in leadership positions that allow them to assert control, protect others, and create meaningful change.

Enneagram 9: The Peacemaker

- **Dream Jobs**: Mediator, Counselor, Nature Conservationist, Photographer, Massage Therapist, etc
- **Why**: Peacemakers are drawn to careers that foster harmony, empathy, and a sense of balance.

Conclusion

Our personality is the blueprint not only for understanding ourselves but also for discovering our purpose. By aligning with careers that resonate with our core motivations, we position ourselves to live with greater clarity, fulfillment, and impact.

Personality Awareness equips us with the tools to recognize these patterns and make intentional choices. When we know ourselves deeply, we can find a career path where our personality, purpose, and passion converge—leading to a life that feels profoundly meaningful.

Chapter 7: Meet Your Guide for Better Mental Health

Personality Health: A Pathway to Mental and Emotional Resilience

As we bring together all the insights from this journey, there's one more critical element of Personality Awareness to explore—**personality health**. More than just an understanding of who we are, personality health provides the foundation for our mental and emotional resilience. It's the state of mind that shapes how we approach life, challenges, and relationships. And because our personality health is fluid, it fluctuates with our thoughts and can be actively cultivated to bring us a healthier state of being. With the tools of Personality Awareness, we gain control over our thought-life, empowering us to guide ourselves to a place of mental clarity and emotional balance.

At the heart of this journey is the realization that personality health isn't about eliminating difficult feelings or experiences. Rather, it's about recognizing patterns in our thinking and making conscious, healthier choices that elevate our mental and emotional resilience. This chapter will show you how to understand the levels of personality health and use Personality Awareness as a guide to shape your mindset and emotions.

Understanding the Levels of Personality Health

Each of us experiences a spectrum of mental and emotional states, and Personality Awareness defines this spectrum into five distinct levels. These levels help us identify where we are and give us a map for moving toward healthier, more resilient states.

1. **Distraught**: This is the lowest level of personality health, where thoughts feel heavy and self-critical, dominated by worry, sadness, or fear. In this state, our actions may become reactive, and we can feel cut off from our natural strengths and resources.

2. **Struggling**: Slightly above Distraught, this level is still dominated by negative thinking, but with glimmers of hope or energy. Here, doubts and irritations may cloud our outlook, but we have a faint awareness of the possibility for change.

3. **Stable**: In this balanced state, thoughts are a mix of highs and lows, and we manage challenges with a fair perspective. It's a place where most people spend their time—a stable middle ground—though it leaves room for further growth and fulfillment.

4. **Healthy**: At this level, thoughts are constructive and positive, and we feel a sense of optimism, clarity, and energy. In the Healthy state, our personality strengths naturally emerge, helping us accomplish goals with greater ease and confidence.

5. **Flow State**: This peak level is where we feel our best. Here, thoughts are purposeful, adaptive, and aligned with our values. In Flow State, creativity flows, setbacks feel manageable, and resilience is abundant. It's the state of mind where we can bring our full selves to whatever we pursue.

Each of these levels reflects how our mindset and emotions shape how we see the world and interact with it. The higher the level, the more adaptable and empowered we feel. With Personality Awareness, we gain a guide for moving upward through these levels, helping us improve our personality health and mental resilience.

How Our Thought-Life Shapes Mental and Emotional Resilience

One of the most powerful aspects of Personality Awareness is the realization that our thought-life directly impacts our mental health. Consider someone facing a difficult setback, such as a personal loss or career disappointment. In the initial stages, their thoughts may be clouded by discouragement, doubt, or frustration—placing them in a Distraught or Struggling state. However, by choosing to focus on constructive thoughts, such as what they can learn from the experience or the support they have around them, they may gradually move into a Stable or even Healthy state. Over time, with resilience, they could reach Flow State, where they feel empowered to grow and thrive despite the setback.

This example illustrates a universal truth: while we can't always control life's circumstances, we do have control over our thoughts. Through Personality Awareness, we learn to choose thoughts that uplift us, enhancing our emotional resilience. As we practice this, it becomes a tool for improving our mental and emotional well-being.

Guiding Yourself Toward Healthier Thoughts

Personality Awareness provides a step-by-step method for guiding ourselves toward healthier thoughts and stronger emotional resilience. Here's how you can use this approach to enhance your personality health:

(Using the Personality Health Chart)

1. **Identify Your Current Level**: Reflect on your recent thoughts. Are they self-critical, balanced, or optimistic? Recognizing the tone of your thoughts is the first step to understanding where you are on the personality health spectrum.

2. **Select a Higher-Level Thought**: Based on your current level, choose a thought that aligns with a higher state. If you're feeling Distraught, focus and meditate on a thought that helps you move to the Struggling or Stable mental state, like practicing gratitude or seeking a positive perspective. If you're at Stable, select a thought that inspires hope or motivation to bring you to Healthy. (All examples are given on the Personality Health Chart according to personality type)

3. **Notice the Emotional Impact**: As you practice this, observe the changes in your emotions. Healthier thoughts often bring relief, optimism, or a sense of purpose, which helps strengthen resilience.

4. **Practice Consistently**: Over time, this practice becomes more natural, helping you stay at higher levels of personality health even during challenging moments.

Each Enneagram type has unique thought patterns, so understanding your personality type offers even more insight into this practice. For example, if you're a Type 5 (Investigator), shifting from overly critical thoughts to ones focused on appreciation or openness may help bring a sense of calm. If you're a Type 2 (Helper), nurturing thoughts of self-worth may feel especially grounding.

Personality Health Chart

Personality Type	Levels of Health				
	Distraught (Unhealthy State)	**Struggling (Low-Health State)**	**Stable (Moderate-Health State)**	**Healthy (High-Health State)**	**Flow State (Optimal Health)**
Type 1 (The Reformer)	**Common Thoughts:** ◦ "Nothing I do will ever be good enough." ◦ "The world is a mess, and it's up to me to fix it." ◦ "If I let my guard down, everything will fall apart." **Emotional Impact:** ◦ Overwhelmed, resentful, and trapped in self-criticism.	**Common Thoughts:** ◦ "I need to work harder to make this perfect." ◦ "Why can't others see what needs to be done?" ◦ "Mistakes are unacceptable and ruin everything." **Emotional Impact:** ◦ Frustration, rigidity, and anxiety over perceived flaws.	**Common Thoughts:** ◦ "I can do my best and trust the process." ◦ "Mistakes are part of learning and growth." ◦ "I care about improving things, but I don't have to do it all alone." **Emotional Impact:** ◦ Balanced, hopeful, and open to collaboration.	**Common Thoughts:** ◦ "I can channel my passion for improvement constructively." ◦ "People are doing their best, and I can guide without judgment." ◦ "Perfection isn't required; progress is beautiful." **Emotional Impact:** ◦ Fulfilled, compassionate, and energized by progress.	**Common Thoughts:** ◦ "I trust myself and others to create positive change." ◦ "The world is beautifully imperfect, and I can embrace it with grace." ◦ "I'm aligned with my purpose and inspire others through my example." **Emotional Impact:** ◦ Peaceful, inspired, and deeply connected to their values and purpose.

Personality Health Chart

Type 2 (The Helper)	**Common Thoughts:** ○ "If I'm not helping, I'm not worth anything." ○ "No one appreciates all I do for them." ○ "I have to give more, even if I'm exhausted." **Emotional Impact:** ○ Overwhelmed, resentful, and deeply insecure about their value.	**Common Thoughts:** ○ "If I say no, people will stop loving me." ○ "I must stay needed, or I'll be forgotten." ○ "Taking care of others is more important than my own needs." **Emotional Impact:** ○ Anxious, overly self-sacrificing, and fearful of rejection.	**Common Thoughts:** ○ "I can care for others without neglecting myself." ○ "It's okay to say no and set boundaries." ○ "People love me for who I am, not just what I do for them." **Emotional Impact:** ○ Balanced, warm, and capable of healthy relationships.	**Common Thoughts:** ○ "Helping others brings me joy, but it's not the only way I matter." ○ "I can be vulnerable and let others support me too." ○ "Boundaries help me give from a place of abundance." **Emotional Impact:** ○ Fulfilled, self-assured, and deeply compassionate.	**Common Thoughts:** • "I am worthy of love and connection simply for being myself." • "My care for others is an extension of the love and care I give myself." • "I inspire and empower others by living authentically and generously." **Emotional Impact:** • Joyful, nurturing, and fully aligned with their purpose of fostering connection and love.
Type 3 (The Achiever)	**Common Thoughts:** ○ "If I fail, I'm worthless." ○ "I have to keep up appearances at all costs." ○ "No one can see the real me because it's not good enough." **Emotional Impact:** ○ Exhausted, anxious, and trapped in fear of failure or exposure.	**Common Thoughts:** ○ "I need to achieve more to prove my worth." ○ "People only value me for my success." ○ "Slowing down means falling behind." **Emotional Impact:** ○ Stressed, overly image-conscious, and disconnected from authentic feelings.	**Common Thoughts:** ○ "My worth isn't tied to my accomplishments." ○ "I can take a break without losing momentum." ○ "People appreciate me for more than just what I do." **Emotional Impact:** ○ Balanced, optimistic, and open to vulnerability.	**Common Thoughts:** • "My goals align with my values and passions." • "Success is meaningful when it serves a greater purpose." • "I can share my authentic self and inspire others." **Emotional Impact:** • Empowered, confident, and deeply connected to their true self.	**Common Thoughts:** • "I am valuable for who I am, not just what I do." • "My achievements reflect my authenticity and purpose." • "I inspire others by being real, not perfect." **Emotional Impact:** • Fulfilled, authentic, and at peace with both success and self-expression.
Type 4 (The Individualist)	**Common Thoughts:** ○ "No one understands me." ○ "I'll never be enough or find where I belong." ○ "Why can't I be like everyone else?" **Emotional Impact:** ○ Isolated, despairing, and consumed by envy or self-pity.	**Common Thoughts:** • "I need to be different to matter." • "People don't appreciate my depth." • "I'll never find the beauty or purpose I long for." **Emotional Impact:** • Melancholic, self-absorbed, and yearning for connection yet resisting it.	**Common Thoughts:** • "My uniqueness is a gift, but I don't have to prove it." • "I can create beauty even in ordinary moments." • "It's okay to feel deeply and still engage with life." **Emotional Impact:** • Thoughtful, emotionally expressive, and open to relationships.	**Common Thoughts:** ○ "I can embrace my emotions without letting them define me." ○ "My creativity connects me to others and the world." ○ "My worth isn't tied to being special—it just is." **Emotional Impact:** ○ Inspired, authentic, and connected to a sense of purpose.	**Common Thoughts:** • "My uniqueness enriches the world, but I'm also part of something greater." • "I create and live authentically without fear or envy." • "I can find beauty and meaning wherever I am." **Emotional Impact:** ○ Joyful, deeply creative, and at peace with themselves and their role in the world.

Personality Health Chart

Type 5 (The Investigator)	**Common Thoughts:** • "I need to withdraw completely to protect myself." • "I'll never know enough to feel competent." • "The world demands too much from me." **Emotional Impact:** • Overwhelmed, isolated, and consumed by fear of inadequacy.	**Common Thoughts:** • "I have to hoard my energy and knowledge to survive." • "If I share too much, I'll lose control." • "People will only drain me if I let them in." **Emotional Impact:** • Detached, defensive, and emotionally distant.	**Common Thoughts:** • "I can engage with the world without depleting myself." • "Sharing my insights helps me connect with others." • "I'm capable of handling life's demands." **Emotional Impact:** • Balanced, curious, and cautiously open to connection.	**Common Thoughts:** • "My knowledge and insight can make a difference." • "I'm enriched by relationships, not drained by them." • "It's safe to be vulnerable and present in the world." **Emotional Impact:** • Inspired, connected, and energized by their intellectual and emotional contributions.	**Common Thoughts:** • "I am both capable and connected, and my insights serve a greater purpose." • "Knowledge is meaningful when shared and applied to life." • "I'm secure in myself and open to the world's possibilities." **Emotional Impact:** • Fulfilled, deeply present, and at peace with their dual needs for solitude and connection.
Type 6 (The Loyalist)	**Common Thoughts:** o "I can't trust anyone, not even myself." o "Danger is everywhere, and I'm not prepared." o "I'll never feel safe or secure." **Emotional Impact:** o Paralyzed by anxiety, suspicion, and overwhelmed by fear.	**Common Thoughts:** • "If I rely on others, they might let me down." • "I need to overthink everything to stay safe." • "I have to stay loyal even if it's not good for me." **Emotional Impact:** • Anxious, indecisive, and overly dependent or distrustful.	**Common Thoughts:** o "I can prepare for the future without being consumed by fear." o "I trust myself to make wise decisions." o "I can rely on others while maintaining my independence." **Emotional Impact:** o Cautious but confident, supportive, and practical in facing challenges.	**Common Thoughts:** o "I can face uncertainty with courage and resourcefulness." o "It's okay to trust myself and others." o "I'm capable of handling whatever comes my way." **Emotional Impact:** o Courageous, self-assured, and deeply loyal in a healthy, balanced way.	**Common Thoughts:** • "I am secure in myself and trust life's process." • "I can find strength in both my community and my inner resilience." • "Uncertainty is an opportunity to grow and adapt." **Emotional Impact:** • Confident, calm, and empowered to face life's challenges with grace.
Type 7 (The Adventurer)	**Common Thoughts:** • "I need constant distraction to avoid feeling pain." • "If I slow down, I'll get stuck in negativity." • "I can't face hard emotions—they'll overwhelm me." **Emotional Impact:** • Frantic, escapist, and consumed by fear of being trapped in discomfort.	**Common Thoughts:** • "If I stay busy, I won't have to deal with hard feelings." • "I need to keep my options open in case something better comes along." • "Commitment feels like a trap." **Emotional Impact:** • Restless, scattered, and unable to find satisfaction.	**Common Thoughts:** • "I can find joy in focusing on what's in front of me." • "It's okay to commit to people and experiences." • "I don't need to run from discomfort—it's part of life." **Emotional Impact:** • Optimistic, present, and able to balance fun with responsibility.	**Common Thoughts:** • "Joy comes from embracing both the highs and lows of life." • "I can fully commit to people and projects that matter to me." • "Facing challenges helps me grow." **Emotional Impact:** • Fulfilled, adventurous, and deeply engaged in meaningful experiences.	**Common Thoughts:** • "I can savor life without needing to chase endless possibilities." • "True freedom comes from being grounded and present." • "I can find beauty and purpose in every moment, even the hard ones." **Emotional Impact:** • Grounded, peaceful, and joyfully present in life's fullness.

Personality Health Chart

Type 8 (The Challenger)	**Common Thoughts:**<ul><li>"I have to control everything or I'll be vulnerable."</li><li>"People are weak, and I can't trust anyone to have my back."</li><li>"If I let my guard down, I'll be betrayed."</li></ul>**Emotional Impact:**<ul><li>Aggressive, defensive, and driven by a constant need to assert power and control.</li></ul>	**Common Thoughts:**<ul><li>"If I show weakness, people will take advantage of me."</li><li>"I need to push people away before they can hurt me."</li><li>"I have to take charge in every situation to feel safe."</li></ul>**Emotional Impact:**<ul><li>Overbearing, mistrustful, and controlling. Feels isolated and on edge.</li></ul>	**Common Thoughts:**<ul><li>"I can stand my ground without shutting others out."</li><li>"I can be assertive and still show empathy."</li><li>"I am strong enough to let go of control and trust others."</li></ul>**Emotional Impact:**<ul><li>Empowered, balanced, and confident without being domineering.</li></ul>	**Common Thoughts:**<ul><li>"I can lead with strength and also be open and vulnerable."</li><li>"My power comes from helping others rise, not just from dominating."</li><li>"I trust myself and the people around me to handle what comes next."</li></ul>**Emotional Impact:**<ul><li>Courageous, self-assured, and deeply connected to both strength and compassion.</li></ul>	**Common Thoughts:**<ul><li>"I lead with purpose, and I trust others to share the responsibility."</li><li>"I can be both powerful and gentle, knowing my worth without proving it."</li><li>"True strength lies in vulnerability and connection."</li></ul>**Emotional Impact:**<ul><li>Grounded, magnanimous, and authentically powerful without the need for dominance.</li></ul>
Type 9 (The Peace Maker)	**Common Thoughts:**<ul><li>"I can't deal with all the conflict around me."</li><li>"It's easier to ignore problems than face them."</li><li>"I'm not important enough to make waves."</li></ul>**Emotional Impact:**<ul><li>Withdrawn, disengaged, and overwhelmed by the chaos around them. Feels disconnected from themselves and others.</li></ul>	**Common Thoughts:**<ul><li>"If I just go along with others, I can keep the peace."</li><li>"Avoiding conflict is the only way to be happy."</li><li>"I can't deal with confrontation—it drains me."</li></ul>**Emotional Impact:**<ul><li>Passive, complacent, and emotionally distant. Struggles to take action or assert their needs.</li></ul>	**Common Thoughts:**<ul><li>"It's okay to voice my opinion, even if it causes discomfort."</li><li>"I don't need to please everyone to feel at peace."</li><li>"Taking small steps can bring me the inner peace I seek."</li></ul>**Emotional Impact:**<ul><li>Balanced, peaceful, and willing to engage without fear of upsetting others.</li></ul>	**Common Thoughts:**<ul><li>"I can create harmony by being true to myself."</li><li>"I trust myself and others to work through differences in a healthy way."</li><li>"I can make my voice heard without fear of conflict."</li></ul>**Emotional Impact:**<ul><li>Harmonious, grounded, and confident in their own worth and ability to navigate challenges.</li></ul>	**Common Thoughts:**<ul><li>"I am at peace with myself, regardless of external circumstances."</li><li>"I can create harmony by embracing both my own needs and the needs of others."</li><li>"I have the strength to face conflict and stay true to my values."</li></ul>**Emotional Impact:**<ul><li>Calm, centered, and fully present. They radiate peace and are able to navigate life's challenges with grace.</li></ul>

Personality Health: A Guide for Resilience and Well-being

Through Personality Awareness, we gain the tools to actively improve our mental and emotional well-being. This journey isn't just about self-discovery—it's about developing resilience in the face of life's challenges. As we improve our personality health, we can handle setbacks with greater ease and continue growing stronger, more adaptable, and more in tune with ourselves and others.

Personality health is the foundation of our mental and emotional well-being, helping us navigate life with a positive state of mind. By understanding and improving our personality health, we not only support our personal growth but also build a foundation for a life of purpose and fulfillment.

Personality Awareness is a lifelong journey of growth and resilience. It's not just about discovering who we are; it's about becoming the best versions of ourselves. With each step, we gain the strength and clarity to live a life of fulfillment, purpose, and joy. Let this awareness be the guiding light on your path, empowering you to face each day with resilience, clarity, and connection.

Chapter 8: Meet the New YOU 2.0

Witnessing Your Subconscious Autopilot

Congratulations—you've reached the final chapter of this journey into *Personality Awareness*. By now, you've glimpsed your subconscious autopilot in action, and if there's one truth you've likely realized, it's this: once you've seen it, you can never "un-see" it.

This awakening is profound. It marks the beginning of a transformative journey—a lifelong process of peeling back layers of unconscious habits, assumptions, and patterns. You've started to notice blind spots you didn't even know existed, and with each revelation, you've gained new levels of clarity.

Understanding your subconscious autopilot is not a one-time event; it's an ongoing journey. Every step brings greater insight into the inner workings of your personality and how it interacts with the world. As you grow, you'll discover that each layer of awareness uncovers another opportunity for growth. This is the art of becoming more conscious—a journey of awakening to your fullest potential.

Revelations from the Enneagram

One of the most powerful tools on this journey has been the Enneagram. It has given you a roadmap to understanding not only your own personality but also the personalities of others.

The Enneagram has revealed how deeply interconnected we all are. It has shown you the patterns that drive your decisions, emotions, and relationships. It has illuminated the strengths and struggles unique to each personality type, offering a profound sense of empathy for others.

But the Enneagram is more than a tool for self-awareness—it's a pathway to a deeper connection with others. By understanding the core motivations and fears of those around you, you can approach relationships with a new level of maturity, transparency, and compassion. This kind of understanding isn't just life-changing—it's relationship-changing.

Centers of Intelligence: Bridging the Human Divide

While the Enneagram reveals the nuances of personality, understanding the centers of intelligence elevates this awareness to an even higher level. Knowing whether someone operates from the head, heart, or gut transforms how we relate to one another.

Without even knowing someone's Enneagram type, simply recognizing their primary center of intelligence allows you to bridge the biggest human divide—the way we think. Logical thinkers (head), feelings-based thinkers (heart), and instinctive thinkers (gut) often feel worlds apart in their approach to life. These differences can lead to misunderstanding, frustration, and even conflict.

But imagine a world where these differences were understood and embraced. What if logical thinkers could appreciate the emotional depth of heart-centered thinkers? What if heart-centered thinkers could value the pragmatic decisions of head-centered thinkers? And what if gut-centered thinkers could see their instinctual responses as a gift, not a flaw?

This is the evolution we need for better relationships. The more we bridge these divides, the closer we come to a world built on understanding and harmony.

The Purpose in Every Personality

Every personality type has a unique purpose. Just as a body needs different organs to function, society needs the distinct strengths of each personality to thrive.

Our personality is our unique fingerprint for how we engage and imprint on the world. Learning about your type isn't just about self-discovery; it's about recognizing the role you were designed to play in the bigger picture.

Whether you're a natural leader, a creative thinker, a nurturer, or a problem-solver, your personality carries a special purpose that no one else can fulfill. By leaning into your strengths and understanding how they contribute to the world, you become an integral part of a well-functioning society.

This is why *Personality Awareness* matters. It's not just a tool for self-improvement—it's a guide to unlocking your potential and finding your purpose.

Personality Health: Self-Care for the Mind

As we've explored throughout this book, personality health is the foundation of mental and emotional well-being. The *Personality Awareness Levels of Health* offer a roadmap to understanding where you are on this spectrum and how to move toward stability, health, and flow.

At its core, personality health is about self-care—specifically, the care you give to your thoughts and emotions. The thoughts your personality repeats on autopilot have a direct impact on your emotional state. When you take control of your thought patterns, you take control of your mental and emotional health.

Choosing intentional thoughts is a powerful practice. It allows you to regulate your emotions, shift your mindset, and step into a healthier version of yourself. By paying attention to your inner dialogue and consciously choosing thoughts that align with your goals and values, you create a positive feedback loop that enhances your overall well-being.

Inspiring Growth and Transformation

You are now on the journey to becoming the best version of yourself. Through *Personality Awareness*, you've gained tools to understand your subconscious autopilot, unlock the revelations of the Enneagram, bridge the divides between centers of intelligence, and embrace the unique purpose of your personality.

This journey is one of growth, self-discovery, and transformation. Each step brings you closer to the *new YOU 2.0*—a more self-aware, emotionally balanced, and relationally mature version of yourself.

Imagine what your life could look like if you continue to apply these principles. Imagine the depth of your relationships, the clarity of your purpose, and the peace that comes from living in alignment with your truest self.

You've already taken the first steps. Now, the rest of the journey is yours to embrace.

Let this book be your launchpad into a lifetime of self-discovery and growth. The new YOU 2.0 is waiting—step boldly into it.